Adult coloring book

BY

TATIANA BOGEMA (STOLOVA)

Our group in facebook:
Tatiana Stolova (Bogema)

Hi! My name is Tatiana and I'm painter :)
Thank you so much that you are choosing my books in spite of many other books present on market. I really appreciate this. Every time I start new project I think about how to make my book more interesting. And I can't do this without you. To do that I need to have your feedbacks. Communication with you is very very important for creation process. With your feedbacks you give me new ideas and inspiration for new books that become better and more interesting.
Sincerely yours, Tatiana.

Nice Little Town Christmas 2 - Adult Coloring Book

Copyright © 2018 by Tatiana Bogema (Stolova)

ISBN: 978-1727226683

THIS BOOK BELONGS TO

NOV 1st 2022

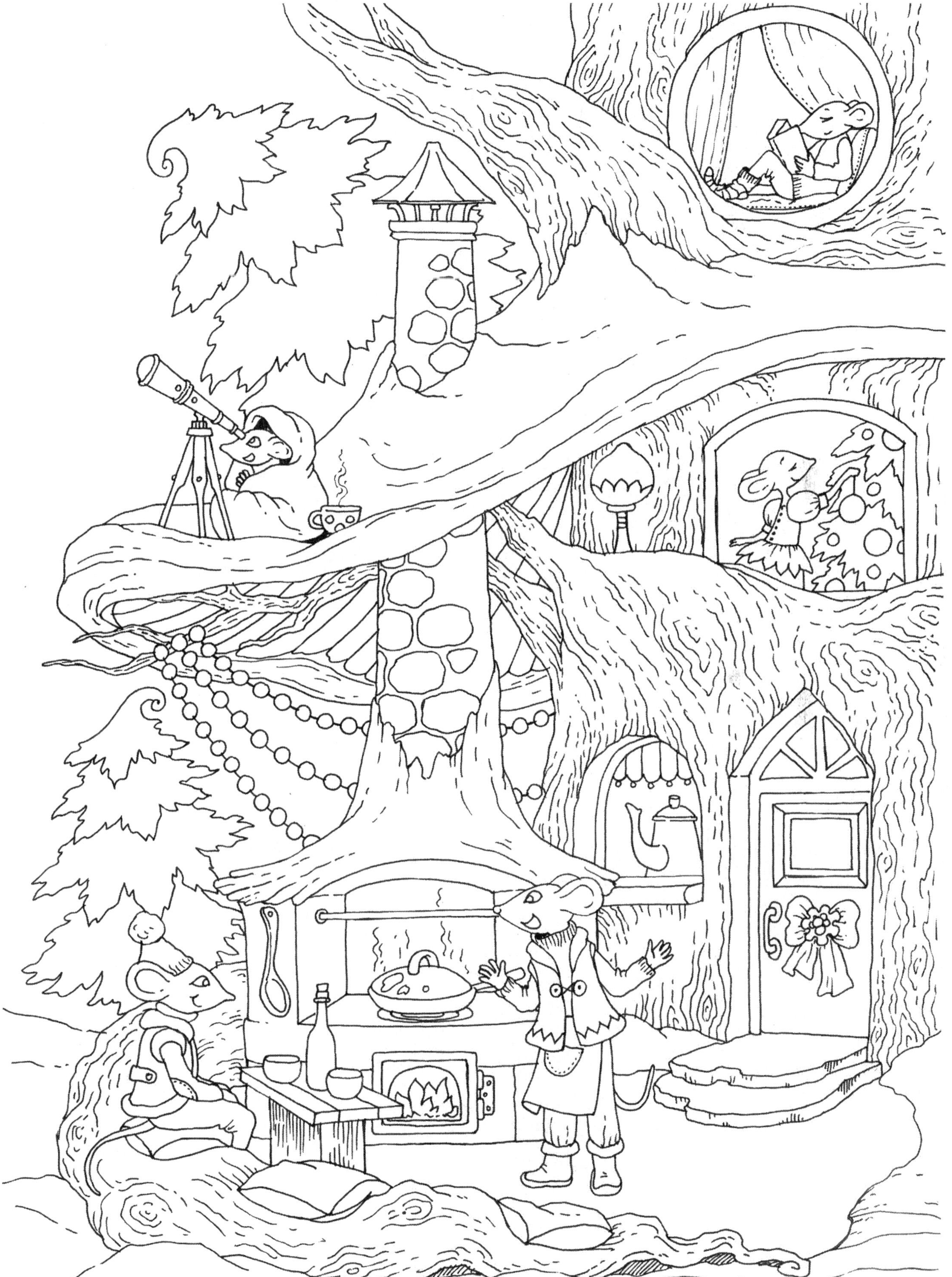

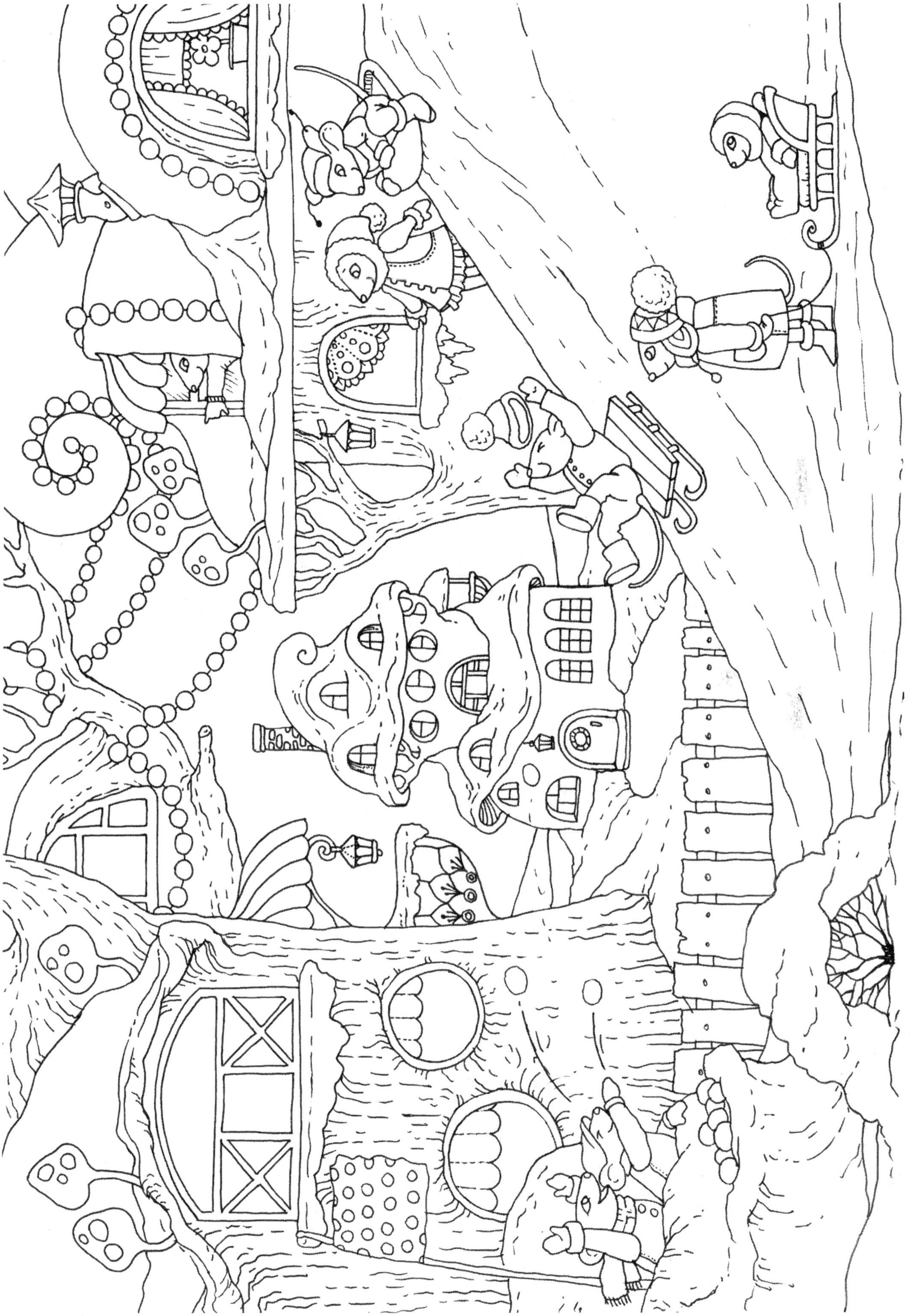

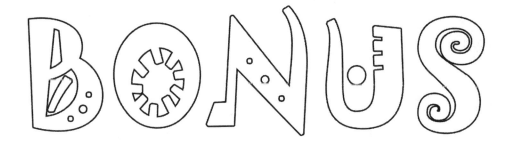

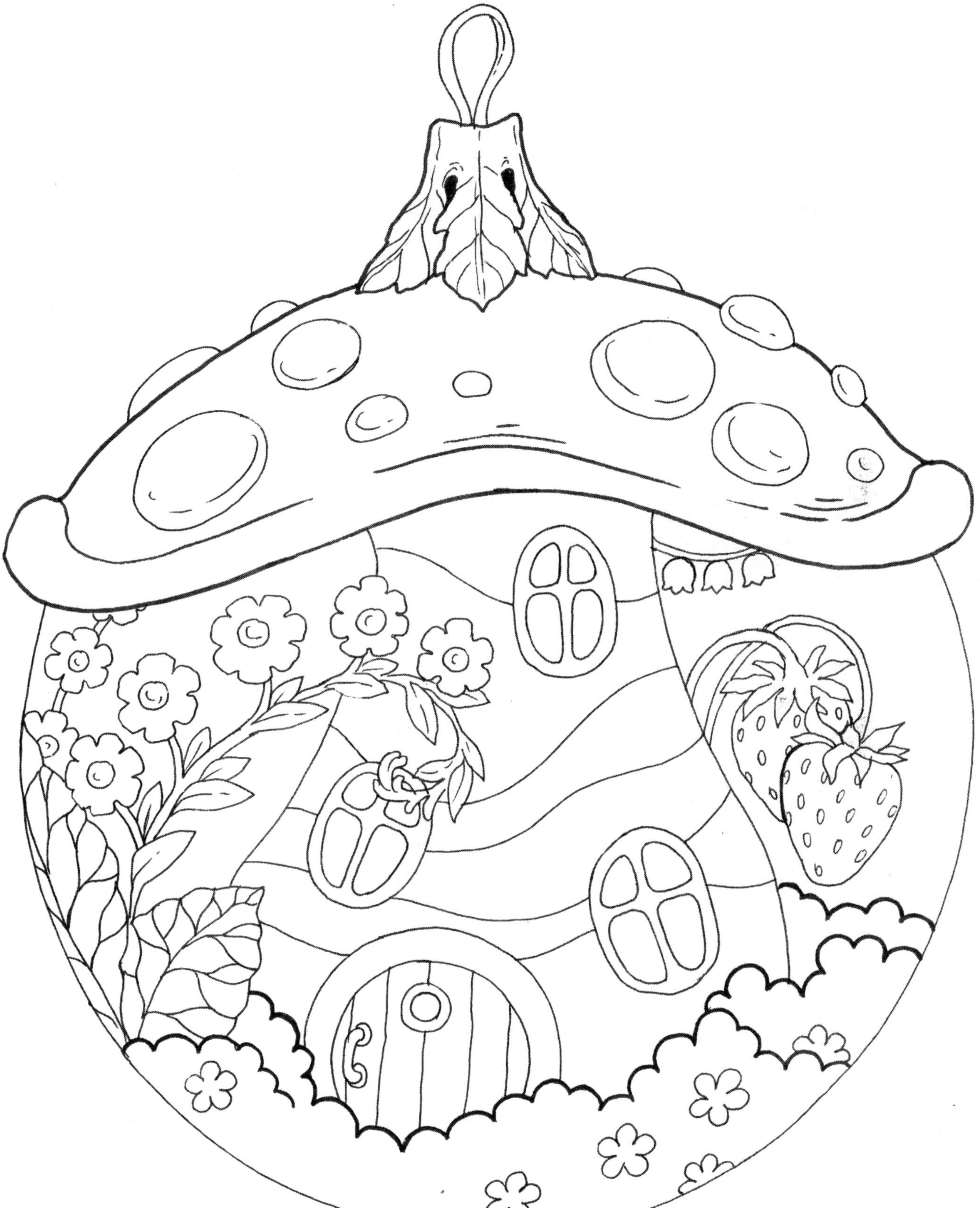

OTHER MY BOOKS

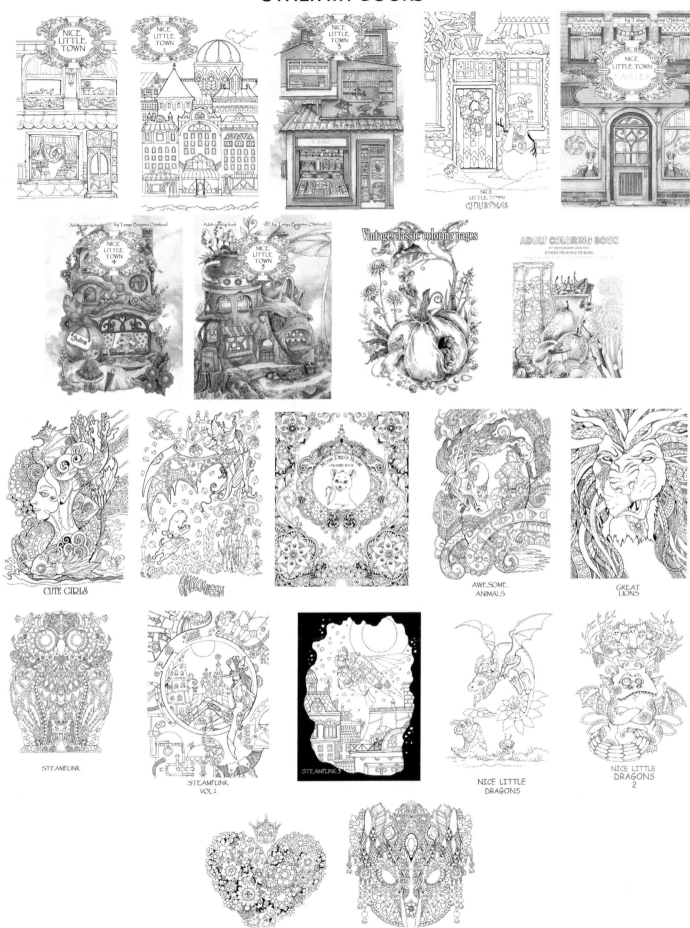

NICE LITTLE TOWN

NICE LITTLE TOWN 2

NICE LITTLE TOWN 3

NICE LITTLE TOWN CHRISTMAS

NICE LITTLE TOWN EASTER

NICE LITTLE TOWN 4

NICE LITTLE TOWN 5

Vintage classic coloring pages

ADULT COLORING BOOK

CUTE GIRLS

HALLOWEEN

AWESOME ANIMALS

GREAT LIONS

STEAMPUNK

STEAMPUNK VOL 2

STEAMPUNK 3

NICE LITTLE DRAGONS

NICE LITTLE DRAGONS 2

FOR VALENTINE, WITH LOVE!

MAGIC MASK

Made in the USA
Columbia, SC
31 October 2022